T0193443

This is My Body and These are My Parts

Written by
Talia M. Newman

Illustrated by
LaVan Anderson

Order this book online at www.trafford.com
or email orders@trafford.com

Most Trafford titles are also available at major online book retailers.

Printed in the United States of America.

ISBN: 978-1-4907-4354-7 (sc)
        978-1-4907-4353-0 (e)

Trafford rev. 08/06/2014

 www.trafford.com

North America & international
toll-free: 1 888 232 4444 (USA & Canada)
fax: 812 355 4082

For my son, Kai, and all the children
around the world.

Your body is special and mine is too.

Our bodies can help us with everything we do!

3

My body is different from your body that's true.

Some body parts on me
are different than on you.

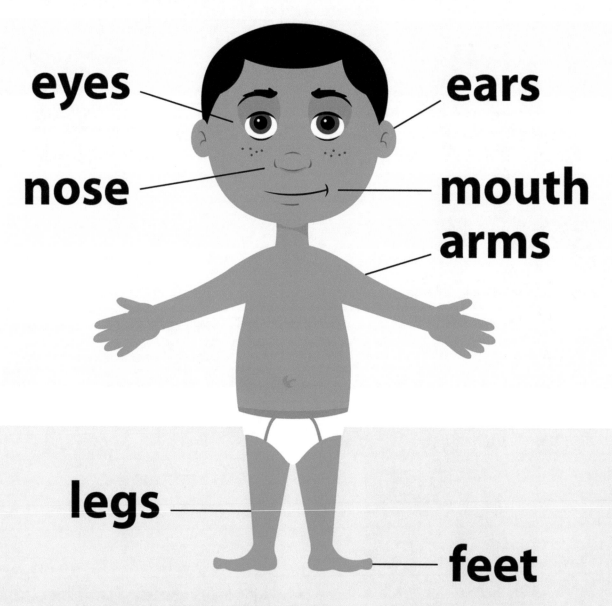

eyes

ears

nose

mouth
arms

legs

feet

I have arms, legs, eyes, ears, a mouth and a nose.

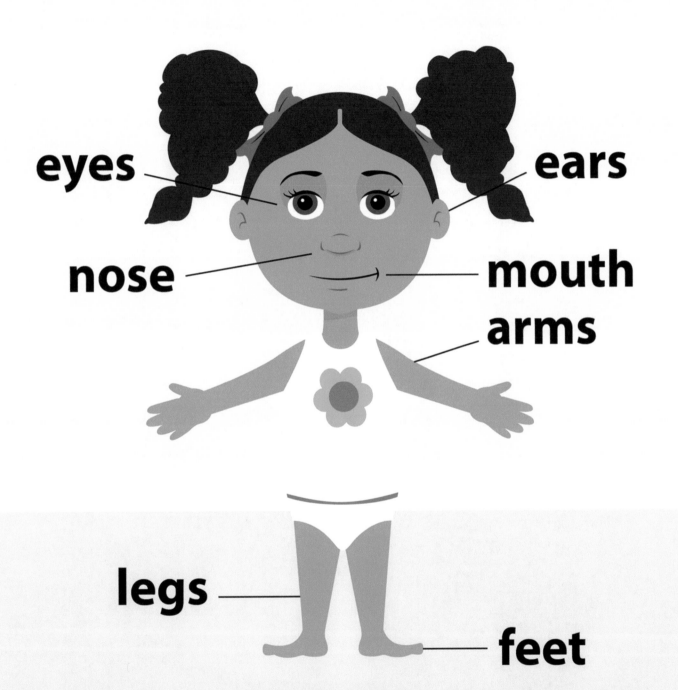

eyes

ears

nose

mouth

arms

legs

feet

But, some parts of my body are private and covered by underclothes.

Private means that it is only for you and not for another. It's something that cannot be shared . . . just ask my mother!

8

Private parts can't be
shared with anyone at all.
Not at school, the
playground, a house,
or a mall.

You should never show these body parts even if someone tells you that it's a secret and asks you to promise that you will keep it.

Some things you may share with your family and a friend,
but NOT your body parts. They are not to lend!

Your private parts belong to you,

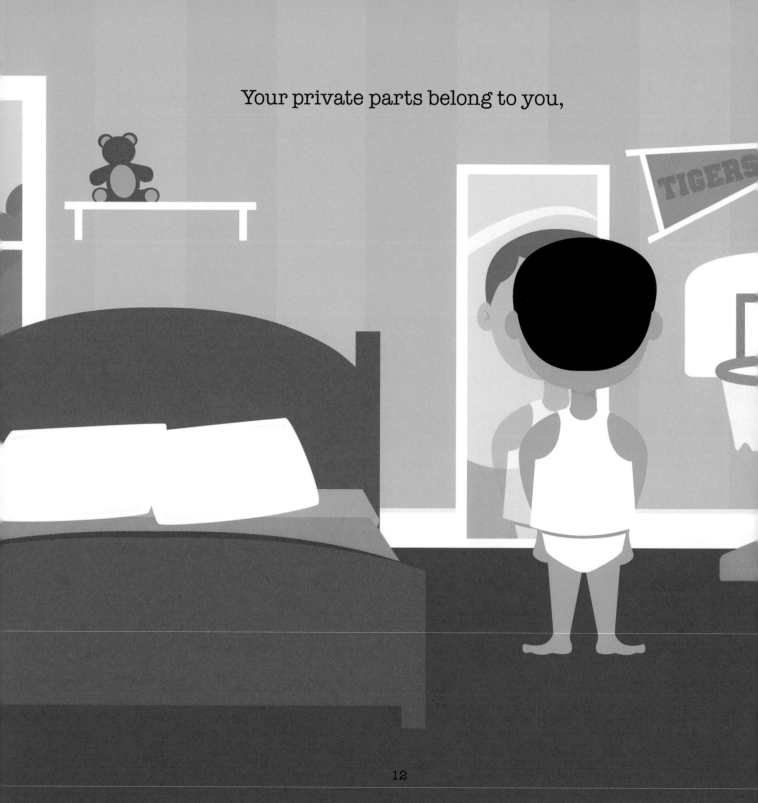

and aren't for anyone else to see.

Except your doctor, who may need to check your private parts to make sure your body is growing healthily.

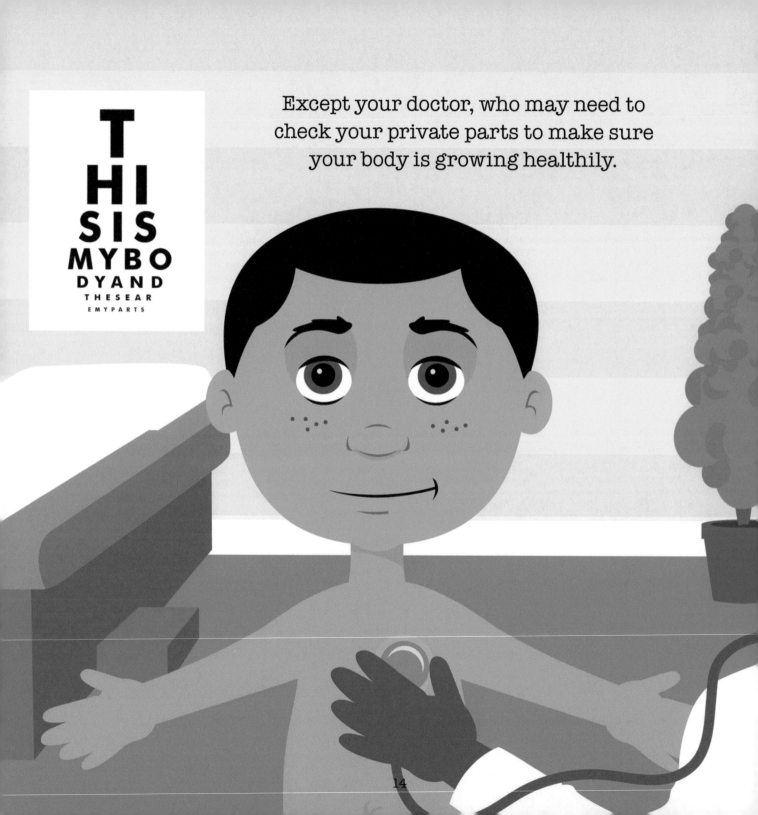

If someone ever asks to see or touch your private parts, shout "NO! These are MY private parts" if they ask why, yell, "Because I said so!"

Be sure to tell a parent, teacher, doctor or someone you can trust. If someone tries to touch you on your private parts, telling someone close to you is a must!

16

Your body and private parts belong to you! Be sure to keep your private parts private and not for anyone else to view.

Printed in the United States
By Bookmasters